AF255814

Tales of Telemachus

Tales of Telemachus

by

STEVE LANG

RESOURCE *Publications* · Eugene, Oregon

TALES OF TELEMACHUS

Resource Publications
An Imprint of Wipf and Stock Publishers
199 W. 8th Ave., Suite 3
Eugene, OR 97401

www.wipfandstock.com

PAPERBACK ISBN: 978-1-6667-6563-2
HARDCOVER ISBN: 978-1-6667-6564-9
EBOOK ISBN: 978-1-6667-6565-6

VERSION NUMBER 022123

*For
Siena
Atticus
Columba*

Contents

Acknowledgements

Many thanks to those who first published, or recognised, individual poems in this collection as follows:

The Galway Review—*Occasionally*

California Quarterly Review—*On a Fine May Morning*

Shortlisted for the Bridport Prize—*Black Hole*

Allegro Literary Magazine—*And Breathe . . .*

Preface

Telemachus was the son Odysseus abandoned, together with his mother, Penelope, on Ithaca, to fight in the Trojan wars, before then undertaking his decade-long, epic journey to return home. When the pressure of the suitors to win his mother's hand, and thereby Odysseus' estate, finally became too much, Telemachus heeded the advice of Mentor, the goddess Athena in disguise, and set out in search of his father.

Prologue

Too coy the haiku- Horatian the ode,
A villanelle reels- a limerick's too light;
A little lugubrious, for me, the ballad,
Too desperate to soar the elegy's height.
No, to page and poet, a blessing's the sonnet-
Witness Dante, Shakespeare, Milton, Petrarch-
An incensed chapel, pregnant silence on it,
Framing so aptly the clear Divine Spark
Of Spenser and Hopkins, Larkin and Donne,
Yeats, Heaney, Shelley, Frost, Keats and Gray,
Their temples high-built, sweet oratories sung.
So, for clarion truth and harmony pray,
Like Blessed Emily's, both keen and strong,
In this "dark world and wide,"[1] for a little song.

1. Milton: Sonnet 19

The Space Between

The crescendo creak of the door
And the slam;
The howling shriek of the brakes
And the crash;
The slip, the frenzied scrabble
And the thud.

For the innocent, the distance from "Defendant"
To "Not";
The slide of your first lover's
Pants down her thighs;
Conceding support of your firstborn's head
To the welcoming palm of her papa.

This silence between my question
And your answer…

Ellipsis

Constellations in chrysalis
Spiral elliptically,
Mute in amniotic motion,
Millions of years old
By now;
All I know is,
As my tiny sliver
Of time
Diminishes,
I sigh more often than I used to,
Tear-up, seemingly at random,
Not with regret, though there's some of that,
But at the crushing pointlessness
And beauty of it all . . .

Faith

Everything
Known
Is conjecture
Trust
In explanation
Something to hold onto
Guard as fiercely as a spoilt child's toy
Deadpan
The blank ring confounds us
Its scope a mystery
Earnestly we
Square the circle
Our angles not right at all
For this specific kind of randomness

Limitless
Is
What it has to
Be
Immortality
Isn't an equation
Reframe the questions in new language
Follow   π
With more humility
Let your mind dilate
To admit
Truth beyond logic
However clear it seems to you
The ends of your circle do not meet

Infinite
Coil
Disappearing
One
Dimension more glints
Its ghostly filaments
Shimmering in the veins of the three
The hole
Appears round but is deep
Zero measureless
Powerful
Inviting entrance
To your narrowing wormhole that blooms
Blooms coincident here but not now

Telemachy

There swelled a sense of loss,
Of bereavement,
Like a rising mist,
That slowly betrays
The breath-taking breadth
And depth of the chasm,
Or a rip-tide
Pulling me farther from shore,
The awful distance
So soon insurmountable;
His legend no longer comfort enough,
To salve the ache,
To assuage the absence,
To absolve my mother.

In my callowness,
The rap of my staff
Rang hollowly
On the dusty floor,
Summoning only shaming tears
And pity for myself;
Like motes of ash drifting
From my own hearth,
At Ithaca,
I seem to be disintegrating;

Meanwhile my bought ship
Waits endeavourless for me,
In the drizzle,
At the end of the runway.

Reborn,
Reinvented;
From one warm harbour,
Borne tender on a watery dream,
Starlit, to silently
Enter another,
Carefully, ever so
Gratefully,
Consummated by the welcome;
To carouse with other men and fools,
Hear him lionized round the fire,
Find wisdom in my host's haverings,
Earnest or pompous,
Set my heart on Sparta.

Was it the hero's humility,
Not just to forgive,
But to fall in love,
Again, with the woman who spurned him?
Or perhaps, as a paragon of *xenia*,
Generosity's apogee,
He sealed in me the wisdom,
To be able to spurn his fine horses with grace,
To know I should be at home, in Ithaca,
And could face, and surmount,
What lay there, without him,

That soon enough, our quests accomplished,
We'll drink together, with no need of words,
From the silver krater of Menelaus.

Posterity

I seem to have mislaid myself,
Which was careless,
To say the least of it;
Not quite sure where or when,
Or, perhaps more importantly, how,
But I feel no sense of connection
With these people in photos I am told are me;
I know who they mean, of course, when they point-
I'd recognize those eyes anywhere-
But I can't see how any of them led to me.

I can't remember how I felt about him,
Wary, I think, as he was, always,
Some part of him unreachable,
But where it came from, the fear of depending,
Giving oneself, is beyond me.

We have a nice terraced lawn out back,
Off-centre, a solitary crag of rock,
Grey, lichen-covered snaggletooth,
Doubtless, millions of years old,
With its clusters of tiny cavities,
Where the molten magma cooled so fast
It caught precisely, for posterity,
The moment of the bubble burst.

Igneous

Acid-tear-scraped, element-carved,
Knist and crack and track and edge,
Gnarl, cleft, crag and facet,
Etched in perpetuity,
Chafed, scoured and sculpted, scriven
Cryptically by lichen colonies,
Remorselessly refined, like character,
Devolving imperceptibly,
At the rate of collapsing stars,
Once globulous flow still implicit,
In this metaphor for stasis,
That draws the warm hand to its mass,
Invites the foot to step up.

Rune

Despoiled, the pallid turquoise,
Speckled half-shell
Perches weightless
On vibrant grass,
Fragile still,
In its brokenness.

Al lado, at an angle,
The unruffled feather,
Slender, *chiaroscuro* blade
Of ash-white, charcoal and powder yellow;

A rune, together, for tragic irony,
Desperation's diphthong-
The empty egg
And fallen feather.

Politicians

A stick of starlings
Lift off the wire,
Circle synchronous,
Arcing dawn's cool air,
Alight in unison,
A flappy revelation,
Reinvented,
From a furious flutter,
Nodding and preening,
On the same lofty perch,
Beginning the inquest into
Who
Twitched
First.

Madrigal

Early morning sun
Bathes me like the milk between
Cleopatra's thighs

Spring Equinox in Tazumal

When the forty days are done,
And dawn's milk spills placid on us,
Sprawled, sex-dazed and intertwined,
By all means reach in and tear out my heart,
To anoint, pulsing yet, the lips of Ixchel,
Fling it, with a flourish, at the star of your choice,
Trailing my blood like a comet's tail;
Bear down, through the fire of my ferocious screams,
Flay me alive[1], turn me inside out,
Then kick my carcass down the purpled steps,
To the lazy jaguars skulking below;
But when flaunting my blemished skin, still warm,
In these streets I played in as a boy,
Be sure to dance in it with all your heart.

1. The poem references aspects of the Mayan civilization's traditions of
human sacrifice

Shellac

They say there is a "Douai walk,"
Ordained by years of negotiating
Treacherous, highly-polished,
Purple and cream tiled halls,
Not ice, (like Bruegel's villagers,
In his distant "*Winter Landscape*",
Disporting themselves on the frigid beck,
Closely observed, from their naked quire,
By two sceptical, cassock-black crows,
With the lethal, "deadfall" bird-trap,
Off-centre, yet somehow ineluctable)
But still, requiring steadiness,
Vigilance,
Restraint.

So, in our self-contained, beetling way,
Each sheltering in his shellac tunnel,
We ply corridors in scaly chrysalis,
Eyes down to the dreaded Study Hall,
Where, in my designate deadfall desk,
I stash febrile, scented love-letters
And dutiful, flimsy airmails,
Then ghost alone to my dorm
In burnished, burgundy brogues
Barely holding on
To unforgiving surfaces,
My spirit hanging

On unseen nails,
Miraculous, beneath the veneer.

Cucaracha

Sleek and scaly,
Bronze-black, like a bullet,
Flattened and tapered,
To slip through evolution,
Improbably cunning,
Scoper and scavenger,
Cruising counter-tops, scouring cupboards,
Scanning for crumbs with your comic antennae,
Then, caught unawares in the cutlery drawer,
Freezing guiltily-
"What's the time, Mr. Wolf?"
Madcap scuttling for corners and crevices
Belies confidence in your
F-fecundity.

Dragonflies

Two dragonflies joined
In coitus in dashing flight
Elation defined

Hummingbird

Hummingbird hovers
Heart beats indiscernible
Jade nectar junkie

Ruin

Shaman, siren, shape-changer,
Winsome, sweet-spiced wisp,
A ravishing ribbon of vanilla-clove,
And mesmerising musk,
Sashaying out of Circe's kitchen,
Seductive as silk
And strict as pheromones,
Thrilling as the coquette's glance,
And toxic as all hell.

"At the tent flap sin crouches"[2]

"At the tent flap, sin crouches", faithfully,
Hunched low and still in dawn's feeble light,
A shadow, like the stump of some ancient tree,
Fingering the fine ashes in his cold, clay stove,
Entranced to sift their silky vanishing,
Mind burnishing still the glowing ember,
The urgent rhythm of our night's long love-making,
He scrupulously self-flagellated to;
Till, finally, I part the folds of our sanctuary,
Blade hot in its sheath against my thigh,
"Master!" he marvels, as I emerge,
Entreaty blatant in his shocking blue eyes,
"Only this, I pray, tell me, where is my brother?"

2. Alter. *The Five Books of Moses*

Mighty

Mighty Thor's hammer, *Mjolnir-*
Or Loki's ancestral *Laevateinn?*
Black Panther's vibranium dagger-
Or Ghost Rider's flailing *Hellfire Chain?*
Tina Minoru's, *The Staff of One-*
Or Thanos's infinity gauntlet?
Maybe Star-Lord's element gun-
Or perhaps Shayera's Nth metal belt?
No, not even the *Heart of The Universe,*
With its mastery of time and entity,
Wielded by the Celestial Order,
Can rival the overwhelming force,
Or match the sheer ferocity
Of the love I have for my brother.

The Bastard

*For Roque Dalton, revolutionary, and El Salvador's greatest
poet, who was sentenced to death three times, the last
resulting in his brutal execution, together with his friend
Pancho, by his own, so-called, comrades, falsely accused of
complicity with the Americans during the civil war.*

The bastard son of your father's nurse,

Battering on your typewriter

With two accusing forefingers,

Prodding you and me and them,

That fucker ██████,

And Poetry herself;

Digging your own way out

When your cell-wall collapsed in Cojutepeque,

After the earthquake in '65,

Excavating Roque

With your nails, a spoon and some chicken bones;

So deep and diligent your disrespect,

Like a caver, pressing stubbornly on,

Through ever-narrowing, cold, dark rock,

Pausing only for two seismic tremors,

Till your headlight conceives

The spacious truth,

Impregnates with light the virgin vault,

A cascade replenishing the crystal pool,

Rhymes the halcyon air to song;

With a knowing glance,
You break bread with Pancho,
Three pieces laid out reverently,
There, on the rose-red-tinted stone.

Through

Through all these layers:
The years, this screen,
That lens, the reflection,
The polished glass,
The dreadful distraction
Of the wide, brown bloodstain,
I'm transfixed by the smallness
Of the single bullet-hole,
Spellbound
By its permanence.

Petition

Petition popes and presidents;
From your humble bedroom, broadcast the brutality,
List the thrashings, threats and torture,
Report the rapes and disappearances,
Itemise murders and martyrdoms.
Ponder with friends the piety of a priesthood
For Martyrs and machinators alike,
Remembering, ever, Rutilio.
So, celebrate sacred Mass for the Carmelites,
For the patient physicians
And their hopeless cases;
Preach, then open your arms to invite
The single, sanctifying shot
That broached your over-burdened heart.

L' Affaire

Shatter my sacred sword on your knee;
Throw the futile pieces to the floor in disdain.
Degrade me, exile me, vilify me;
On your devil's island, bind me in chain.

Array your slippery evidence-
Lie, forge, smear, collude-
To entangle me, in your oily clench,
In the inky depths of your turpitude.

But, I transcended your arrogance,
And, bathed in the light of the aurora sun-
"A moment of human conscience"[3]
Fought for you, vindicated, at Verdun.

---

3. Zola. *J' Accuse*

Resilience

Post-rain softness brings
Grackles down to yank up worms
Somehow unbroken

Water

Before He created heaven and earth,
There was water;
His spirit shimmered over its face,
And, yes, it moved to His command,
To accommodate sky,
Hold back for earth,
To promulgate life,
And most prodigiously,
But before light and firmament
Sun, moon and stars,
Before flora and fauna,
Even you,
And our love,
Just water.

Rescue

The rescuer should punch the drowning man
Full-force in the face, to stun him, they say,
Quell him, even better, knock him out,
For fear his furious, terrified thrashing
Injures his would-be redeemer,
Or worse, his desperate death-clench
Pinions his saviour so they both go down;
I'm okay with that-
So long as I reawaken to the strong, reassuring
Clasp of your hand below my chin,
The purposeful sound of your trained breathing,
The power and reach of your long, strong stroke,
The sight of sailing, moonlit clouds,
And the amused stars winking between them.

The Saviour

*Written on the 5th anniversary of the day on which John
Ogden Nash Jr (Nobel Laureate and schizophrenia suf-
ferer), and his devoted wife Alicia, died together in a tragic
car crash on the New Jersey Turnpike, on May 23rd*

Thirty-three,
A child is born
On New Year's Day,
Alicia, meaning, "Of noble character".

16 of 800, as a percentage, is two,
And, as a young woman, she was one,
At MIT, added to their number,
And John Forbes Nash Jr.
Was her irrational Other;
The manifold genius,
As complex and elusive as
Equilibrium,
And as handsome a bundle of fibre
As a girl could hope to reconcile.

"Devotion" is a word not much used these days,
To a Catholic, it's "an expression of love and fidelity";
And, "commitment" means something else entirely,
When your husband is diagnosed
Schizophrenic,

And then, by addition, for perdition,
Your son.

Shakespeare's mercy is one thing-
Twice blessed- it's true to say,
But true compassion
Is double its worth,
Reckoning on no reciprocation,
Ergo, a perfect
Analogy for love.

El Mozote

What can you hear from your tree, Rufina?[4]
The air, chopped in dud clumps,
Pulse up the lush valley,
Remorselessly, maniacally;
High-pitched, strained, familiar voices,
Mothers mainly, calling for children,
Rising dread and desperation
Tightening their throats,
The thrash of brush, crack of branches,
As the Atlacatl broach the undergrowth;
A barked order, commotion,
A frantic scurry,
Ragged tear of an M16 volley,
Pause of the universe at the vulgarity.
A scream:
The first of two days of screams,
Still swirling and rising and echoing,
With the moans of the raped girls,
Atrocious, sky-splitting cracks of the rifles,
Sudden silence.

What can you smell from your tree, Rufina?
Nitroglycerin.
Burnt flesh.
Sick sweetness of crushed, overripe mangoes;

That evening, wood fires and bean stews,
As in cantons across the land,
But the air laced too
With the slick curl of cheap ron,
The sweat of soldiers,
And the comforting stench of your terror.

What can you see from your tree, Rufina?
At dawn, toddlers swinging from neighbouring trees,
Such heavy fruit,
Each one, an American bullet saved.

What can you taste in your tree, Rufina?
The blood of your own
Chewed lips.

What can you feel in your tree, Rufina?

4. Rufina Amaya was the sole survivor of the El Mozote massacre of Dec. 11th and 12th, 1981, during the El Salvador civil war. She hid from the government soldiers in a tree, from which she observed the rape, torture and slaughter of her family and friends.

"When none can call our power to account"[5]

"Yet who would have thought
The old man to have so much blood in him,"
Laughs the leader of the Little Angels,[6]
Boasting of the single shot
With which he bisected the mute congregation,
Patient doctors and their hopeless cases,
Parsing the long aisle's incensed air
And the widespread arms of the poor man
Copying Christ on the cross behind him.

5. Shakespeare. Macbeth

6. "The Little Angels" is the name of the death squad believed to be responsible for the assassination of Monsenor Oscar Romero, while he celebrated Mass at a palliative care hospital, that sparked the beginning of the civil war in El Salvador.

Ix Chel

Here are my cold, stone hands outstretched,
To welcome your fluttering, still-beating heart;
And here the strict, sacred womb of my chalice,
To plash purple, engorge with your slick, sticky warmth;
Oh, the thrill of it, thrill of it, thrill of it!

Swagger

With a languid lick, I cherish my claws,
Heinous, hooked, glittering, pearly dirks,
As hard and sharp as sheen obsidian,
So facilely to unfasten skin,
Cinch, at my clench,
Sweet purchase in flesh,
Bright-white excruciation,
Exhilarating in my tightening clasp;
Ah! To savour sinking into you,
Then lash out, in a raking blur,
Your entrails on the dewy grass,
This urge, the glint
In the depths of my blank eye,
Insouciance in my sashay, my swagger.

Yearn

Yearning to be perfected,
To be redivined,
To want nothing, finally,
Have nothing to prove,
To be forever in a fragile
Moment of grace,
The poignant dewdrop
At the tip of the blade,
Bending light,
Defying gravity,
Suspending time,
Potential burgeoning,
Unspoilt, unspent,
Yearning to be no more

Security

Security is one:
The things I lock or close or check,
After you thought I was safely in bed;
And cleaning,
The way my soapy hands
Affirm, each one, the other, and me;
The twist and grist of the pepper grinder;
The savoured scenes and dialogues-
Juicy-bright, sweet, tempting jewels-
Like Willy Wonka's gobstoppers.
Traditions like "Grace" and "Ladies First,"
My brother forgetting to feed the fish;
These are my anchors,
The tethers that tense
At the gentle, but insistent, tug,
The impulse to soar
Obliquely,
Yet, so soon so high,
In ether so thin, so exhilarating-
Ozone so rare, so scantly blue;
What works for you?

You

You reach up and out
Higher and wider
In your wild ambition
For light and air
To be lit and warmed
There where you easily
Spread and soar
Flower and fruit
Shade and shelter
Admired from afar
Not me
I plunge down
Deep down and in
Muscling deeper
By fibre and sinew
Thrusting blindly through
Stone and bone
Dark moist earth
The humus of here
The deeper the darker
The warmer the tighter
The safer
Grappling myself to our garden
And you

A Figure of Speech

I'm only too aware of its treachery,
This matted kelp in olive-green clumps,
Sliming slick the mute, black rocks
I stumble over or labour around;
I'm sometimes tempted to reach in and lift
And weigh the wet, blank tangle of tapes,
But, appalled by their unctuous, fleshy strands,
Or what may lurk, malicious, beneath,
Or that they might spring to life with a screech,
And lash flat tentacles round my wrists,
I press on, head down, for the harbour,
Where neatly tethered boats give solace,
And there's respite, finally,
From the articulate wind.

And Breathe . . .

If you
Happen
To be suspended
In the north-east Pacific
Spiriting yourself around
In the amniotic half-light
Helpless and exhilarated
A blue whale swimming
At cruising speed
Takes fifteen
Seconds
To pass you
Bearing her precious calf
And her thirteen ancient songs

Frown

My frown is now fixed,
Regardless of my mood or context,
Two asymmetric, scythe-shaped trenches,
Carved between my eyes,
Haphazard apostrophes,
Marking some omission,
Perhaps a legacy of long years
Squinting in the tropics,
Or too many pretending
To be cleverer than I am;
But, glancing again,
In the rear-view mirror,
I see that I've just been
Forever perplexed

Occasionally

Occasionally,
Very occasionally,
At least for me, arrives
That feeling of wanting
To be nowhere else,
My heart being full
To that point, at which,
I am careful it shouldn't spill over,
That, in itself, should tell you something;
But even more
Should the rarity of it,
For which, in truth,
I have no-one to blame
But myself.

Hammock

My empty hammock
Draws the very same ellipse
As my closed eyelid

Blue

My eyes are a mere reflection,
A coherent scattering of light,
A figment of your perception,
No pigment clouds their sight.

If I'm Honest

If I'm honest
I shouldn't really
And it's not like me
To be fair
I don't know what comes over me
It's not like I make a habit of it
Believe it or not
But there it is
For good or ill
There's no denying
And when everything is said and done
Truth be told
I really shouldn't
If I'm honest

Gioiosa

Last night, live,
On Channel 4,
A transgender comedienne,
Ripped off her clothes
Apassionata,
And played the piano
With her organ *colossale*
(Mano sinistro, apoyando);
Surely a defining
Interpretation
Of *con brio,*
A piacere,
Eroica,
Brava!

Assurance

Insinuating certainty,
Was ever the trite traitor to me;
Quick and glib, so slick and blithe,
Declaring smugly death and the tithe
Alone to be sure in this universe,
Yet how universal now seems hubris;
Nurses may be depended on,
The sycophant leers craven,
Cocksure assertions and pontifications,
Predictions and facile proclamations,
Even ugly prejudices,
Slip the lips of the careless,
Who lecture us all, but never learn,
That the only sure thing is being wrong.

The Foolish Man

And the rain came,
And the floods fell,
And the foolish man
Was bound with cords,
And with due process
Impaled upon
The upturned horns
Of the altar.

4/12/20

Irony

What is it with you and the endless practice,
The countless keepie-ups in your Gola boots,
Relentless free-kicks blasting the blank wall
Behind bamboo goalposts you'd jiggered together,
Misses grabbed gingerly from the snake-ridden copse?

Look at you, socks round your ankles like Jinky,[7]
Hands on hips, one foot on the scuffed ball,
Squinting through African sun and sweat,
Defiance blazing in your blue, Scottish eyes.

Practice makes perfect- is that what they told you?
Listen to me, you arrogant wee nyaff,
Practice makes confidence
And confidence is king,
But only God and irony are perfect.

7. Jimmy Johnstone: famous Scottish footballer

Skirl

Swirling and curling and keening
Down timeless, gun-grey,
Rock-strewn glens,
Their rushing burns, *con brio*,
Glitter, audacious and ice-cold,
Under the lour of overbearing bens,
Battle-dread thrum of the doleful drone,
Plaintive paean tempered
By whisky-bright whirls of the seductive chanter,
Sweetened with scent from each
Bruise of heather;
Bosie of brotherhood, coorie of kinship,
Reveille to recall we're yet
Scots wha' may.

The Future

The future is something I worry about a lot.
Perhaps that explains my sleeplessness,
Perhaps not;
That's one thing not among my worries-
Night-time, for me, is liberation,
Freedom finally from your endless questions,
Your judgments and your expectations,
Your relentless, ant-like obsession
With socializing interaction,
To feed your need for affirmation.
But, at dead of night, you join me alone
With your thoughts and your imagination.
What happens to me, when mum and dad go,
Is what worries me most, if you really must know.

Athena Mentors Telemachus

Head-born, bright-eyed, wiser at once
Than mild Mentor, the fool, whose failing form
She assumed, to assure the trust of Telemachus,
Divine intervention, the wisdom of a woman,
To inspire the ingenue, educe the epiphany,
Commission his own quest, of the sallow son,
But the father, found finally, is home ahead of him,
Stiff bow strung taut, feathered bolt, in flight,
Cleaves the hot curtain of Ithaca's clear air,
Whispering as it passes through the axe-heads' eyeholes:
"Believe the beggar, who belies the legend!"
Sweet the shrill song of the swords unsheathed,
A votive quivering, below the observant owl,
Announcing annihilation, the slaughter of the suitors,
From Antinous and Amphinomous, to the progeny of Prolyctor,
Proci sprawled lifeless, the ravishers ravaged,
Their vacant eyes validate the legend's legacy,
Leaving me, lonely son, to my many ignominies.

Icarus

So detached, my feathers
Dwindle down, twirling,
Lost overblown snowflakes,
In a Titan sky,
Till, wheeling, ungainly,
A macabre doll flung,
I plunge, screaming, through them,
Hastening to my fate:
Rock hard embrace
Of the glittering sea
And eternal ignominy,
The height of hubris,
Long forgotten, the grace
Of my valiant flight.

Being Telemachus

Thomas, I'll surely serve as your searcher,
When October comes again, again;
While, James, I could have been Hamlet for you,
But you favoured 'Dedalus'[8]; I see now the draw
Of the labrynth builder, the wingsmith's hubris,
And the tragic gift of the sonslaughter.
I posed primly for your tapestry, Carole;
For you, Louise, I'm a trope for torpor,
Or a fucked-up family (my mother faking
The shroud, father absent, fondling his legend;
Me, with the goddess's tongue in my ear).
And, grateful as I am for your gilt allusions,
Somehow, I never quite earned my own complex,
Though, trust me, I don't envy Oedipus his.

8. Joyce. *Ulysses*

On a Fine May Morning

Its heft in my hand feels momentous,
My heart, bizarrely, all first-date nerves,
As the scope and scale
Of this map of dark matter,
That scythes through stars and souls and secrets-
Hers and mine and yours- is manifest,
And I am faced with the start
Of my very own epitaph:
"Firstborn, (1968).[9]" Unnervingly,
"On a Fine May Morning"[10] repeats on the radio-
"She'll sew no silken seam," it seems;
But the poet lay down in lush grass with her Lover:
Giving humbly, like generous earth, to his roots,
Taken gently, like light and water from air.

9. Gluck. *Poems 1962–2012, section 1 title page*
10. Traditional English folk song

Recessional

56

You're in the blue adidas coaches' coat
I bought you, that you loved so much,
Though (bless you!) the sleeves were far too long,
One hand, as ever, in your trouser pocket,
The other holding your grandson's hand,
Given to you without word or care,
Offered up freely to vouch for you,
A year or so before we knew
About him, and the same before you died,
Toddling off quietly away from me,
Lit together, in the damp, winter night
By an instantaneous flare of trust,
Instinctive as his first breath,
And decisive as your last.

Admission

However you care
To look at it,
I left the door open,
Didn't I?

Other books by Steve Lang:

Heavenly Hurt: Utafiti Foundation, 2016
ISBN 978 9966 26 091 8

Cuarentena: Resource Publications, 2021
ISBN 978 1 6667 1658 0 (Paperback)
ISBN 978 1 6667 1659 7 (Hardcover)
ISBN 978 1 6667 1660 3 (EBook)

Bibliography

Gluck, Louise. *Poems 1962–2012.* New York. Farrar, Straus and Giroux, 2012, section 1 title page

Alter, Robert. *The Five Books of Moses.* New York. W. W. Norton and Company, 2008